Greene County

A Memoir of Home

BY

NANCY ELLIS-ROBINSON

Copyright (c) 2019 Nancy Ellis-Robinson

All Rights Reserved. This book or any portion thereof may not be reproduced or used in any manner whatsoever without the express written permission of the author.

Table of Contents

Homecoming 1

Weekends In Greene County 4

Train Ride South 8

Family Ties 12

Revival 19

Cousin Adventures 22

Glossary 25

Acknowledgements 28

About the Author 30

Homecoming

The Great Migration, also referred to as the Great Northward Migration, occurred between 1916 and 1970. More than six million African Americans moved from the rural Jim Crow Southern United States to the industrial Northeast, Midwest, and the West. Many African Americans traveled from Alabama, Georgia, Florida, Mississippi and other southern states.

My parents, Reverend William and Susie Allen Ellis, lived in rural Alabama. Their close-knit community was located in the west-central part of the state. In search of a better way of life, my father and mother decided to move north, along with my maternal grandmother, Annie Bell Allen, taking part in the Great Migration.

My parents left their home in rural Alabama, a place known as *Warrior Swamp* in Greene County and eventually settled in Chicago, Illinois. The place they had called home was a small predominately African

Greene County

American county greatly affected by the loss of many of its sons and daughters who had made the decision to move up north. They left to find work in the factories, steel mills, and stock yards. These industries and many others desperately sought the manpower Southern migrants were willing to provide.

The North offered many opportunities to these people, but many returned yearly to their roots. "Going home," became a wonderful seasonal ritual for many Southern migrants. Each summer the highways, Greyhound buses and railways would fill with these pilgrims anxious to return to their native lands. They were often heavily laden with gifts and goodies to share with their Southern relatives.

My sister Janie and I were fortunate to have been a part of that yearly celebration. We always looked forward to the long ride home to my father's birthplace in Greene County, Alabama. What a joy it was to be back in the South! We often played in the dirt, fed the chickens, milked the cows, slopped the hogs, and picked watermelons. We also got to ride in horse-drawn wagons, roll in the hay loft, go horseback riding, and row the canoes.

Weekends In Greene County

Sundays were a special time too, as my father and my uncle were both preachers. Attendance at church and the revival was mandatory. It seemed everyone attended church and my sister, and I loved getting to see our cousins from every part of Warrior Swamp. We were never bored. Not even for one minute!

Arriving in town on a Saturday was so exciting! We'd simply say "hello" to anyone standing on any corner. It wouldn't take long for the word to get out that the city girls were back home. Our cousins and friends would flock over to our uncle's house by the time we'd arrived to greet us.

Church was and still is the hub of the Greene County community. You would see anyone you didn't see during the week at church. The joyous sounds of acapella hymns and rhythmic foot stomping never failed to soothe my heart.

I had the opportunity to visit West Africa as an adult. I realized during this trip that the music of my youth, though quite different from the worship I was accustomed to, was only a few generations removed from our African ancestors.

What a revelation and blessing to know and understand the roots of the rich heritage I'd been born into! Those sweet melodious sounds still resonate within me today.

Greene County

We were all made to feel special in Greene County. My sister and I were known as the cousins from "up North". We were always fawned over and there were no shortages of hugs and kisses. Looking back, it's all the love I always felt from my family and friends that made the home of my youth so memorable. I shall never forget my Alabama roots! It was a magical time and this book is my tribute testament to that wonderful time of innocence, joy and exploration.

My big sister Janie and I could not wait for school to end. The next day we were going home to Greene County, Alabama - the most fun place in the whole wide world! Preparations had gone on for weeks. There were brand new clothes piled on our beds. Momma cooked and wrapped delicious foods for us to take on our trip. She packed each mouthwatering morsel in a shoebox. We always helped Momma pack our overflowing suitcases for our trip. All our friends and neighbors

Nancy Ellis-Robinson

knew we were going, but we made sure to say goodbye before we left!

Train Ride South

The following day we set off for Greene County. Hampton, my big brother, came to pick us up. I could not help but cry a little as the car drove off. I knew we'd be gone a whole month. We always waved to my mother and our grandmother, which we called Big Momma, as they waved goodbye to us on the curb.

Grand Central Station was enormous and filled with all kinds of people. I couldn't wait to get on the train with my family. I waited in line with my sister, and our father with our luggage and the shoe box lunches our mother and Big Momma had prepared for us.

Nancy Ellis-Robinson

The train ride was known as the *Hummingbird*. It was huge! We got on and settled in. The train made a *choo choo* sound as it left the station. There were African American Pullman Porters on board. They looked handsome and dignified in their spotless white jackets. It was their job to tend to the needs of every passenger on the train. They would get someone a pillow, blanket, or even a light for their cigarette! The Pullman Porters were there to make the trip comfortable.

Once aboard, the smell of fried chicken, pork chop sandwiches, chocolate cake and many other delicious aromas wafted through the train cars designated for colored people. All the people in our car had shoe box lunches. My Father explained that it was necessary for us to bring food because African Americans were not allowed to eat in the dining cars.

We'd wake after a good night's rest just as the train pulled into Birmingham, Alabama. Daddy's sister, Aunt

Greene County

Sweet, lived there. We would visit her and her family before heading to the Greyhound bus station, to continue our journey home. There was a *Whites Only* sign dividing the front seats from the back seats when we got on the bus. The back seats were reserved for African Americans. My father would always tell us to keep moving to the back of the bus until we were seated in section marked: *Colored Only*.

It was a three-hour ride to Greene County. The bus would stop along the highway and pick up passengers. It seemed like we would never reach our destination! Finally, the bus pulled into our stop where Uncle Bishop, my father's brother, would be waiting for us. My heart raced knowing we were so close to home! We traveled long country roads and over a very old rickety bridge which ferried us across the Black Warrior River. At long last, we were in Greene County.

Nancy Ellis-Robinson

Janie and I hopped out of the truck and put our luggage down in a hurry. We both kissed Aunt Virga before scurrying off to visit our many cousins and friends. Our summer adventure had begun! Boy, that sun was hot! The sand even hotter, but we didn't care. We were home, ready for all the excitement and fun new experiences sure to take place!

Family Ties

Everyone had a nickname in Greene County. Our first stop was at Uncle Thousand's house, whose real name was James Garfield. He was a handsome man that had been a beautiful baby. In fact, he'd been so pretty that a woman had jokingly offered his mother a thousand dollars for him. His mother had refused, but his nickname stuck! He taught us how to prime the pump to get water from his outdoor pump. Uncle Thousand gave the biggest hugs and he never wanted us to leave!

We visited Grandpa John next. Our grandfather lived right up the road. He'd been born a slave and was a child when slavery ended. He'd told us he'd left the plantation and walked to Greene County after the *Emancipation Proclamation*. He'd been there ever since. I always thought about the plantation he'd been on. I wondered where it was or how far he'd walked to get to the place he called home. Grandpa John was old and blind, but never missed the chance to hug us. We always got lots of hugs at home!

Our cousin Boogie lived across the road from Grandpa John. Her real name was Carrie. She fed us the best vegetable soup in the whole wide world! She always made it from the vegetables she'd grown in her garden. I loved her delicious soup, especially with her hot buttery corn bread. My sister and I had fun with her grandchildren, Ray, Mary Alice, and Carrie. They thought we were funny for not knowing so many things about the country. We'd go exploring different places, happy to hear about all the happenings in Greene County.

The nights were pitch black. The stars seemed close enough to reach out and touch! The crickets sang so loud, I swore they were right outside the door. There was nothing to do at night but sit on the porch and listen to the radio. We'd tune into *Randy's,* a program

Greene County

out of Nashville and listen to country music. Janie and I would swing on the indoor swing on many of those hot muggy nights. We'd often make a pallet on the porch. We'd talk, listen to the crickets, and katydids until we fell asleep. It was just too hot inside!

Aunt Virga fixed breakfast on a big black stove in the morning. She'd put firewood inside of it of every time she cooked. Bringing in logs of wood was also one of our summer chores. It was a lot of work, but her scrumptious homecooked meals made it worth it!

Every Monday we had to wash clothes in a huge black pot. My aunt would fill the pot located under a tall tree full of pumped water. There were mounds of dirty clothes to be washed! My knuckles would burn from scrubbing clothes on the tin washboard. It was hard work, but we had to do it.

Nancy Ellis-Robinson

There was a lot to be done on the farm and I enjoyed helping. Aunt Virga taught me how to milk a cow and churn milk until it became butter. I loved feeding the chickens! They would run to me whenever I started saying, "here, chick, chick, chick," whether I had food to feed them or not.

Some days we would feed or *slop* the dirty hogs. The animals were big and grubby. They smelled awful and made so much noise when they saw us coming with their food. It was fun to watch the hogs gobble the feed Uncle Bishop threw in their pen, but I didn't like to hang around there too long.

Greene County

Our Uncle Thousand owned a cotton patch. We'd pass by its on our way to the watermelon patch. To me, the cotton fields looked like balls of snow swaying. Those fields stretched as far as the eyes could see. I remember saying how beautiful the cotton was, but my Uncle told me I wouldn't think so if I had to spend all day picking it.

Uncle Thousand's House

We rode to the watermelon patch in a horse-driven wagon. There were big beautiful watermelons everywhere! Uncle Bishop let us each pick one of our own. As we traveled over the area, my Uncle explained that our family owned this property. His mother, my grandmother, Nancy Ellis, had willed the land to her family and their children.

Uncle Bishop explained to us how many African Americans entered another form of indentured servitude called *share cropping*. These former slaves had no money, so they lived and worked on the plantations of white landowners for a share of the crops. He explained that the landowners could deduct rent and any credit extended from the sharecropper's earnings. Most sharecroppers rarely benefited from this

Greene County

arrangement. In fact, many often found their "settled account" resulted in debt, not profit.

Uncle Bishop's House

Revival

We could not wait for Saturdays! That was the day our father would give us money for the 5¢ and 10¢ store. My uncle would drive us in his car to town. We would see people on the corners, in the stores or passing by in cars, trucks and wagons. Everyone waved and greeted each other.

There was a beautiful park with a huge gazebo in middle of the town. It had lovely flowers and always looked so inviting. I wanted to go in, sit and enjoy the scenery. Sadly, I was told the park was for White people only, which didn't make any sense to me.

Greene County

On Sundays, we would awake to joyous sound of gospel music playing on the radio and the smell of hot biscuits. The announcer would recite the names of all the people who had died and were funeralized that week. My sister and I excitedly dressed in our new Sunday clothes. We couldn't wait to get to church and see all the people. Sunday was always a special day in Greene County!

The Old Green Oak Baptist churchyard would be filled with wagons, trucks and cars with many people standing outside when we arrived. We could hear the congregation from a distance singing hymns of praise inside. We loved hearing the soulful rhythms of hand clapping and foot stomping as we made our way into the church.

Sundays were great, but the week-long revivals were another story. I found them a little bit frightening as a child. There was a *mourner's bench* for sinners to sit on. The revival was loud and long. The service was filled with moaning, groaning, many prayers, and a powerful sermon directed to young people in an effort to save them from a fiery hell. I was always thankful when the revivals were over, and I did not have to sit on that bench.

Cousin Adventures

We could visit and spend the night with our other cousins after the weeklong revival finally ended. I loved going to visit my cousin Abraham Kennard, and his wife, Cousin Mae Lou. There was never a dull moment with ten young cousins to play with! Their son Abe was my favorite. He liked to hang out with us. Abe would show us the ways of the south. He even taught me how to fish. Mary, his sister, would run the hot comb through our hair. We had so many cousins and all of them provided different experiences while we were at their house. There was always something to do. I had so much fun in Greene County!

We also enjoyed playing with our other cousins, the Slays and the Armsteads. Sometimes, we would spend the night at one of their houses. We shared many great experiences with our family. The fun was non-stop with so many aunts, uncles, and cousins to do things within Greene County.

Nancy Ellis-Robinson

I had many unforgettable experiences in Greene County, but riding a rowboat through the swamp will always be my favorite! It was scary and yet thrilling. There were snakes, turtles, and frogs jumping around. My heart would race hearing all those different sounds! I would cling to the side of the boat and pray to get out safe. I imagined all kind of wild creatures in there, but I never let on that I was scared!

There were no stores close by in Greene County. So, once a week the *Rolling Store* came around. It was like heaven to me and all the other kids. The Rolling Store was a converted school bus filled with candies, ice cream, cookies, chips and other goodies.

The days seemed to rush by in the South. Before we knew it, my father would announce that it was time to start packing. Our adventure filled vacation had come to an end. Where had the summer gone?

Greene County

I was always sad the day my Uncle Bishop drove us back to the bus station. I didn't want my summer vacation in Greene County to an end, but it was time to leave. I never wanted to go, but I knew I would always come back to Greene County. I have never stopped returning home. There is no place, like this place – Greene County!

Glossary

A Capella:

Music sung without accompaniment.

Colored:

Offensive term referring to Black/African American people.

Emancipation Proclamation:

The Proclamation issued by President Lincoln on January 1, 1863, freeing the proclamation slaves.

Gazebo:

A small roofed structure that is screened on all sides.

Indentured Servant:

Greene County

A person placed under a contract to work, without pay for a set period of time.

Myriad:

A great or indefinite number of persons or things.

Migration:

To go from one country, region or place to another.

Mourners Bench:

A bench or seat at the front of the church for mourners or sinners to set on at a religious revival service.

Pilgrim:

A person who travels to a distance

Plantation

Nancy Ellis-Robinson

A large farm of estate usually worked on by laborers.

Randy's Records:

Legendary record store opened in 1946. It became the first to sponsor a primarily Black radio show on a high-powered radio station, WLAC-AM in Nashville, TN. The show could be heard in 20 states.

Revivals:

A religious service for the purpose of effecting a religious awakening.

Sharecroppers:

A tenant farmer who has as rent a share of the crop.

Swamp:

Land that is wet and spongy, often having certain types of trees and other vegetation.

Acknowledgements

To my wonderful husband, Alderson Robinson, who supported me every step of the way. I thank you and bask in your love, approval and assistance. You mean the world to me. I wish the Ancestors could have met you.

I am deeply indebted to my Sister, Janie Ellis Drew Ray, who shared these summers with me and reminded me of some of the incidents I had forgotten. Love you Sis, and this has been quite a journey together, hasn't it?

Sincere thanks to my Sister Friend, Gwendolyn Lee Tyson for volunteering to do the first edit on this book. What a blessing to have a retired English/Reading Specialist for a life-long friend. I can never thank you enough.

Thanks to Almighty God for putting my editor and publisher in my face. I had no idea how to take this project to completion, but my God had gone before me to handle all the details. I am deeply indebted and thankful to Angela Bradley who has earned a special place in my heart.

To my wonderful parents, Rev. William and Susie Ellis, thanks for taking us to Greene County every summer. Thank you for sharing our rich heritage and letting me know who my people are. I miss you.

To the Ancestors, Grandparents, Uncles, Aunts, Cousins, those deceased and those yet alive – I AM because you. You poured so much into me and I have tried to make you proud.

About the Author

Dr. Nancy Ellis-Robinson received her BA from Chicago State University, her MA in Educational Administration and Supervision from Roosevelt University, MA in Inner City Studies from Northeastern Illinois University and an Ed. D. from Loyola University of Chicago.

She was an elementary school teacher and the principal of the Simon Guggenheim Elementary School, in Chicago, Illinois. Guggenheim earned national and international acclaim for its innovative approach to educating children.

Dr. Ellis was a faculty member at Cambridge College, in Cambridge, Massachusetts. She taught and worked in Administration for 20 years in their School of Education. She is published in the Journal of Minority Education, and the author of *Looking for A Party, Interactive Lessons for Children*.

Nancy Ellis-Robinson

In addition, Dr. Ellis is an accomplished musician serving numerous churches in her long career as a church pianist, organist and choral Director. She shares her love of travel with her husband Alderson Robinson. She connects yearly with Greene County Alabama at their annual convention.

Made in the USA
Coppell, TX
02 March 2021